On the second day of Christmas,
My true love sent to me,
Two turtle doves, and
A partridge in a pear tree.

*On the third day of Christmas,*
*My true love sent to me,*
*Three French hens,*
*Two turtle doves, and*
*A partridge in a pear tree.*

# THE Twelve Days OF Christmas

## Ian Beck

**OXFORD**
UNIVERSITY PRESS

On the first day of Christmas,
My true love sent to me,
A partridge in a pear tree.

On the fourth day of Christmas,
My true love sent to me,
Four colly birds,
Three French hens,
Two turtle doves, and
A partridge in a pear tree.

On the fifth day of Christmas,
My true love sent to me,

*Five go*

Four colly birds,
Three French hens,
Two turtle doves, and
A partridge in a pear tree.

On the sixth day of Christmas,
My true love sent to me,
Six geese a-laying,
**Five gold rings,**
Four colly birds,
Three French hens,
Two turtle doves, and
A partridge in a pear tree.

On the seventh day of Christmas,
My true love sent to me,
Seven swans a-swimming,
Six geese a-laying,
**Five gold rings,**

*Four colly birds,*
*Three French hens,*
*Two turtle doves, and*
*A partridge in a pear tree.*

On the eighth day of Christmas,

My true love sent to me,

Eight maids a-milking,

Seven swans a-swimming,

Six geese a-laying,

**Five gold rings,**

Four colly birds,

Three French hens,

Two turtle doves, and

A partridge in a pear tree.

On the ninth day of Christmas,
My true love sent to me,
Nine drummers drumming,
Eight maids a-milking,
Seven swans a-swimming,
Six geese a-laying,
Five gold rings,

Four colly birds,
Three French hens,
Two turtle doves, and
A partridge in a pear tree.

On the tenth day of Christmas,
My true love sent to me,
Ten pipers piping,
Nine drummers drumming,
Eight maids a-milking,
Seven swans a-swimming,
Six geese a-laying,
**Five gold rings,**
Four colly birds,
Three French hens,
Two turtle doves, and
A partridge in a pear tree.

On the eleventh day of Christmas,
My true love sent to me,
Eleven ladies dancing,
Ten pipers piping,
Nine drummers drumming,
Eight maids a-milking,
Seven swans a-swimming,
Six geese a-laying,
**Five gold rings,**
Four colly birds,
Three French hens,
Two turtle doves, and
A partridge in a pear tree.

On the twelfth day of Christmas,
My true love sent to me,
Twelve lords a-leaping,
Eleven ladies dancing,
Ten pipers piping,
Nine drummers drumming,
Eight maids a-milking,
Seven swans a-swimming,
Six geese a-laying,
**Five gold rings,**
Four colly birds,
Three French hens,
Two turtle doves, . . .

...And a partridge

# in a pear tree.

# OXFORD
## UNIVERSITY PRESS

Great Clarendon Street, Oxford OX2 6DP

Oxford University Press is a department of the University of Oxford.
It furthers the University's objective of excellence in research, scholarship,
and education by publishing worldwide in

Oxford  New York

Auckland  Bangkok  Buenos Aires  Cape Town  Chennai
Dar es Salaam  Delhi  Hong Kong  Istanbul  Karachi  Kolkata
Kuala Lumpur  Madrid  Melbourne  Mexico City  Mumbai  Nairobi
São Paulo  Shanghai  Singapore  Taipei  Tokyo  Toronto

with an associated company in Berlin

British Library Cataloguing in Publication Data available

ISBN 0-19-272544-0

1 3 5 7 9 10 8 6 4 2

Printed in Malaysia